THE ANXIETY RELIEF PROGRAM

THE ANXIETY RELIEF PROGRAM

by

Dennis Radha-Rose

Published by
Mushroom Publishing

Copyright © 2004 Dennis Radha-Rose

Dennis Radha-Rose has asserted his right under the Copyright, Designs and Patents Act, 1988, to be identified as the Author of this work

First published in 2004
by Mushroom eBooks

This edition published in 2005 by
Mushroom Publishing, Bath, UK

All rights reserved. No part of this publication may be reproduced, stored in a retrieval system, or transmitted, in any form or by any means without the prior written permission of the publisher, nor be otherwise circulated in any form of binding or cover other than that in which it is published and without a similar condition being imposed on the subsequent purchaser.

ISBN 1-84319-303-5

Printed and Bound by
Lightning Source

Contents

	BEFORE YOU BEGIN	1
1	INTRODUCTION TO ANXIETY	3
2	FACING UP TO ANXIETY	19
3	DON'T WORRY – BE HAPPY!	33
4	COPING WITH PANIC	45
5	PHOBIAS AND COMPULSIONS	61
6	WORKING WITH MINDFULNESS	81
7	THE BREATHING MIND	91
8	YOUR PROGRAM	106
9	LIST OF EXERCISES	112

BEFORE YOU BEGIN

The Anxiety Relief Program is not a substitute for professional attention, but a guide to self-help intended for those who suffer from any form of anxiety to a not overly severe degree. Those whose anxieties and symptoms are acute should take medical advice before doing the Program. The author or publisher cannot be held responsible for the consequences of following any of the suggestions made in this book or of doing any of the exercises in it.

Selecting your program

Read the whole book through before you try any of the exercises. Then, using the questionnaires, identify your symptoms. This will give you a guide to the type of anxiety you have, *though this is not a medical diagnosis.* Then turn to Chapter 8, "Your program" and select those exercises you want to start with. You may want to change them later as you try them out.

Psychic and other illness

If you are having or have had any treatment for anxiety, many of the exercises may not be suitable for you. If under these circumstances you still want to do the program, you should refer to your doctor first. You should also consult him if any anxiety symptoms get worse or new ones appear. If any of the physical exercises gets painful, stop immediately and take medical advice. If you have severe emotional difficulties or other symptoms you should immediately discontinue the program and refer to your doctor.

Medication

The object of the Program is to overcome anxiety and phobias without medication, but if you feel you need it to keep your symptoms under control, consult your therapist or doctor. On no account simply stop the medication without medical advice.

Legal Disclaimer

Any use of the Anxiety Relief Program shall be deemed to be an acceptance of and agreement with the above and constitutes the Contract between the author and the user. This Contract shall be governed by and interpreted in all respects in accordance with the law of England.

Chapter 1

INTRODUCTION TO ANXIETY

Anxiety is a feeling like hunger – it creeps up on you whether you want it or not.

Shirin Ebadi, Nobel Peace Prize winner

What is needed rather than running away or suppressing it or any other resistance, is understanding fear; that means, watch it, learn about it, come directly into contact with it. We are to learn about fear, not how to escape from it.

J. Krishnamurti

Introduction? Who needs an introduction to anxiety? We all have it at least from time to time, and if we didn't we would often find ourselves in threatening situations, for it is a warning signal that something is not right with our world, that there may be something dangerous out there – or worse, *in here,* in our body or mind.

How the program helps you to cope with anxiety

You can't stop the waves of anxiety but you can learn to ride them. No program, medication or therapy will cure a severe illness or change a situation such as your bank account being in the red. External circumstances remain as they are. But what we can do is to change the way in which we react to the situation so that the object of anxiety does not control us, which means keeping ourselves under control. Then we are in the best possible position to cope with the outside situation and improve it as much as it can be. The Anxiety Relief Program will help you to do this. Of course, some anxieties are imaginary, such as that of a person who continually washes her hands because she is afraid they are "contaminated". Here the ARP helps by changing the relationship to the thought of contamination.

Since 9/11 there is a new and appalling cause for anxiety – terrorismdirected against us all. It is all the worse because there is no way to know what will happen next, and we cannot do anything personally to prevent it. But we have to learn to control our anxiety about it so that it will not destroy us.

Sometimes anxiety becomes excessive and to overcome this you need to understand why and how it happens. Although the popular (and not so popular) press often prints lengthy and colorfully illustrated descriptions of the neurophysiology of anxiety, we need not concern ourselves with that here. It is far more important to discover *from our own experience* what gives rise to our anxiety, how we feel it and above all what we can do to overcome or at least cope with it. If you have, say, acute anxiety when you have to board a plane, you will hardly be helped by thinking about what your amygdala, limbic system and other parts of your brain are doing. But you can be helped by the Anxiety Relief Program, therapy or both. It may be early in the book to say so, but though a quick Valium taken at the check-in may help you board the plane, tranquilizers lead to dependence, and so on your next trip you will probably have to take two...

Anxiety is a thin stream of fear trickling through the mind. If allowed to do so, it cuts a channel into which all other thoughts are drained. You can't think of anything except what you fear. It does not help to try to suppress or deny it or merely to try to distract yourself from it. You cannot run away from it because it will follow you wherever you go. You have to face up to it, admitting to yourself that you are excessively anxious and that this can dominate your life. True, you can take tranquilizers to get over a crisis point, but they only work for a limited time and help only with the symptoms. Tranquilizers do not solve the basic problem but cause you to avoid confronting and accepting your anxiety, which is the only way to cope with it. You can go to a therapist, who will be a help, but even he or she will tell you that in the end you must do the actual work of coping with your anxiety yourself.

Anxiety can get you into a vicious circle

Anxiety, if not kept under control, can change from being a thin stream to become a raging torrent, overflowing its banks and sweeping away everything in its path. But you can control it and so avoid the disasters that can result from anxiety. It may only be one particular worry or anxiety that develop into the "General Anxiety Disorder"". It is important to be able to recognize it in its early stages and to take steps to cope with it, otherwise it can paralyze your thinking and make you act irrationally and you will no longer be able to take effective steps to protect yourself from danger. Uncontrolled anxiety can lead to panic attacks, which can begin with a feeling of intense terror and impending doom followed by physical symptoms. Or it can lead to compulsions or phobias, which are unreasonable fears of objects, activities or people, these being quite unrelated to the real cause for the anxiety.

Anxiety brings much physical discomfort. This includes shakiness (both inside and outside), rapid heart beat or palpitations, stomach distress, sweating, dizziness, rise in blood pressure, rapid breathing, and an increase in muscle tensions; the intestinal blood flow decreases sometimes, resulting in nausea or diarrhea as well as numerous other bodily sensations. They are naturally worrying and so can cause further anxiety. Now you are in a vicious circle and have a double problem – you are anxious about becoming anxious! This is one of the paralyzing aspects of anxiety. You can't walk into the elevator or drive your car because you are afraid you will have an anxiety attack – and its accompanying physical symptoms, causing still more anxiety

To get out of this vicious circle an anxious person can learn to raise his tolerance for discomfort and so not get obsessed with the bodily sensations. If you do focus too much on the symptoms you will inevitably become anxious about them and they will dominate your thoughts. You need a change of attitude towards the symptoms and sensations.

Accepting it – "I'm an anxious person"

One of the most important skills one can hope to master in order to bring an anxiety disorder under control is *acceptance*. It can be difficult but is the essential first step in coping with anxiety in all its various forms.

The typical attitude to the physical symptoms of

anxiety is that they are "horrible, terrible things". If you can learn to regard them as merely "uncomfortable" you begin the process of accepting anxiety and so reduce the tension it causes. An example might be having tight and tense jaw muscles. Instead of thinking "This is intolerable", try to see it simply as a passing discomfort – after all it cannot last forever. Acceptance is not approval of what is happening but only the process of rethinking what is going on in your body and telling yourself the truth about your present reality.

Anxiety stops us from doing many things we would like to do (flying is an example) but once you have mastered the skills of proper breathing, relaxation and countering unrealistic thoughts, and practiced graduated exposure in facing your fears, you will no longer be concerned about feeling symptoms of anxiety but will simply be able to do whatever you choose to do as if you had no anxiety and are free of all the restrictions you used to impose on yourself. You can honestly ask yourself if you would do a certain thing if you did not have anxiety. If the answer is "Yes", you can simply do it. This is the ultimate acceptance and freedom from any bonds that anxiety ties you with.

A further level of acceptance is broader and more personal. It requires learning to approve of oneself in a very realistic way. If you are a person with anxiety, it does no good to berate yourself about it. Anxiety is nothing to be ashamed of or to feel guilty over, for we do not have direct control over our emotions. You do not have to keep it a big secret or hide it from the world and there is no need to be ashamed of anxiety – it is something you have in common with the rest of mankind.

The anxiety film

One of the destructive effects of anxiety is that you get lost in it. Your thoughts are so focused on the reason for your fear that you lose all consciousness of "what is going on in your head". What in fact frequently happens is that you make a "film" of the future events about which you are so anxious and run it over and over again. Because you yourself are the script writer, producer and director all in one you can change or add new scenes and details to the film, which gets nearer and nearer to a catastrophe every time you run it. The leading role is always taken by the same player – yourself. But it won't earn you an Oscar, that's for sure.

There are special exercises for stopping the film, and if you are continually running it you should certainly do them.

Stages of the Anxiety Relief Program

The ARP has several stages, though these are not completely separate. It consists of a series of training exercises which you can try out, selecting those which you feel best with. This means that you can construct your own program. There will be a period of trial and error at each stage but you will have the advantage that the exercises you do are suited to your personality and your problems.

Acceptance is the first stage of the Program; acceptance that you are a generally anxious person, preoccupied not only with the objects of your anxiety but with its symptoms as well. You can and should admit this not only to yourself but also to your partner or a trusted friend, but that in itself is not enough. Acceptance is a skill that needs to be learned and this is possible through the second stage exercises.

Breathing exercises. It is a well known fact that incorrect breathing is both a cause *and* a symptom of anxiety, and so the importance of correct breathing cannot be overstressed. Breathing from the stomach rather than from the upper chest reduces the tendency to anxiety and also combats its symptoms. In case you are wondering how this happens, it is enough to say that there is an important nervous connection between belly and brain (ever had "butterflies in the stomach"? – then you'll know). Therefore, to learn, or rather *relearn,* correct breathing is the object of the first exercises. All other exercises should be accompanied by correct breathing.

By doing the Breathing and Movement Exercises, not as mere physical exercises but with a distinct mental attitude, you will learn the skill of acceptance. This attitude is called "mindful awareness" and is an essential basis of the Program – it helps you to find yourself again when you are lost in anxiety.

Mindful awareness. Mindfulness is a process of healing the wounds in the mind which life brings to all of us. It has proved its value over thousands of years and is increasingly practiced today. It originated as the basis of Buddhist meditation but is in no sense a religious exercise; it can be practiced by people of all faiths and beliefs or of none.

In all of us there is a silent observer that keeps track of our mental and physical states, of the contents of the mind (what we are thinking about) and of our feelings. Unfortunately we frequently ignore it, because the quality that it embodies – "mindfulness" – is not generally known in our culture, yet it is an essential tool for coping with anxiety and stress.

Mindfulness stops us projecting anxious thoughts into an imagined and quite likely catastrophic future that can only too easily become a present but illusory reality. It does not dwell on painful memories of the past. It is awareness of what is happening NOW. This is not to say you cannot think about and plan for the future, but rather that you do so in a completely realistic way.

Above all, mindfulness makes no judgments about what it is aware of. It is simply an observer, making no attempt to be a critic of what it sees. If it becomes aware of a thought which causes the feeling of anxiety, this will not be classified as "good" or "bad" but simply noted as a thought which causes anxiety. This allows thoughts to be seen as simply thoughts and not mistaken for the reality you are anxious about. Simply observing a thought, as you would a bird flying by, reduces its power to create negative feelings. This is a very important point, so if it's not quite clear to you please stop and read it over again.

The ARP is largely based on a modern and clinically proven method of stress and pain reduction called "The Mindfulness Based Stress Reduction Program". It was developed by Dr Jon Kabat-Zinn at the University of Massachusetts Medical Center and is used in more than 300 clinics in the USA. It enables you to train yourself to be in control of your anxiety and the stress it brings with it. This happens through the development of the skill of attention and moment-to-moment awareness *without negative reactions* to your anxiety and its symptoms. Mindfulness brings calm and stability. When thoughts or feelings come up in your mind, you don't ignore them or suppress them, nor do you analyze or judge them as either "good" or "bad". Rather, you simply note any thoughts and observe them intentionally but non-judgmentally, moment by moment as they occur. They are simply events in the field of your awareness. Paradoxically, this noting of thoughts and feelings that come and go in your mind and body stops you from getting caught up in them.

Selecting a program for yourself

The first step is to decide, not what you are anxious about, but *what kind of anxiety disorder* you suffer from. It is a *disorder* if it goes beyond the usual anxieties of life and is a disrupting influence interfering with your life and quite possibly making it hell. It could be a specific anxiety, chronic worry, general anxiety, agoraphobia, other phobias or an obsessive compulsion. As you read this book and answer the questionnaires you will recognize your own place in the overall pattern of anxieties. Chapter 8 gives more detail on how to select your program, so that you can then start work. Suggestions are made in the various chapters for sessions in which you do the exercises as described, but no fixed program is laid out. After all, every person has his or her own needs and reactions to the exercises. Just be sure you devote enough time to them. It's an important matter, isn't it?

Read the whole book through before you try any exercises; this is important as it will help you to understand them better. Then make a program for yourself with two weekly sessions (or more). Decide what exercises you want to start with. Try these for a while to see how you get on, then review your progress and how you reacted. Change the exercises if you think it would help and you feel you would respond better. Do the exercises one by one, not several at the same time.

The exercises

There are exercises for each kind of anxiety. For specific and general anxiety, each session includes visualizations, which get to the very core of your problems. You "record" your anxieties on an imaginary videocassette and then you play them back. If your feelings become too strong you press the "stop" button. Otherwise you make the picture smaller and then put the cassette in a safe. Before and after the visualization you do breathing, sitting exercises and Body-Scan, which all develop your mindfulness. They bring calm and relaxation and enable you to look clearly at your anxiety and see what it really is – an illusion, however real it seems. There are also breathing exercises and other exercises that combine breathing and movement.

How long does it take to overcome anxiety?

If you have been living with anxiety in any form for a considerable time, even perhaps from childhood, there's no way you are going to be free of it overnight. Begin at the beginning; read the book completely through to get the general feeling, not skipping to the exercises first. Then work through the chapters again, and when you get to the exercises you need, start doing them as explained.

The platform of the Anxiety Relief Program

The ARP is built on a number of principles which you should follow no matter what form your anxiety takes: specific anxiety, general anxiety, excessive worry, panic, phobia or obsession.

Where there is **trust**, there can be no anxiety. Trust in God if you are a Christian, Jew, Muslim or Hindu. If you are a Buddhist take your refuge in the Buddha. Above all, trust in yourself – *you can do it!* Trust your partner or a friend with your thoughts, fears, anxieties and even terror. The best person to trust is one who simply listens, not one who tries to give you ready-made answers or criticizes you.

Pray for the ability and patience to bring anxiety under control instead of letting it control you. God will give you the ability and patience, but you have to do the work, for he helps those who help themselves.

Develop "mindfulness", that is, **moment-to-moment awareness**. All the exercises will help you develop this essential skill.

Correct breathing is an extremely important ally in healing anxiety and its consequences. Many people breathe faster and faster when they are anxious, and many other bodily functions may get out of control. Mindfulness of breathing enables the body to return to normal.

You are larger than your anxiety. Any form of anxiety, if allowed to do so, comes to dominate your life and limit your horizon. When you have accepted yourself as an anxious person (and who isn't, at least at times?) you will see that this is so and feel the need to reduce anxiety to a corner of your being. You will achieve this through the exercises.

Some lifestyle hints and tips

· Think of activities which calm you and distance you from the circumstances which cause you anxiety.

· Be sure you have a healthy diet, avoid alcohol and drugs (an occasional beer is OK).

· Avoid medicaments affecting how you feel, unless they are prescribed by your doctor. Even when he suggests one don't just grab the prescription and run to the drugstore, but ask about its necessity, risks and side effects. And don't be put off by that white coat!

· Do some relaxation exercises regularly in the morning and before going to bed, because a relaxed body feels no anxiety.

· Physical exercise burns off excess adrenaline and other stress hormones. Anxiety is the mind's response to "fight or flight", which releases stress hormones into the body even when they are not needed. Exercise improves physical well-being and helps to restore mental balance. Choose the kind that you enjoy and can do regularly – jogging, cycling, walking, swimming, dancing etc. *Above all, don't just sit there wrapped up in your anxiety. Do something!*

- Learn how to slow and finally stop the whirl of thoughts. This will come as your mindfulness develops more. On no account try to "empty your mind". This is often suggested but is an impossibility, as new thoughts come one after the other. Just watch them as if they were birds flying by.

Chapter 2

FACING UP TO ANXIETY

NOTE: The exercises with a visualized TV set in this and other chapters should be done without hurrying or forcing yourself in any way to get results. If you don't have success at first, try again in another session.

There is nothing new about anxiety, or to be more accurate, *irrational* anxiety, which is not just a product of our stressed and hectic modern lives. The Greek poetess Sappho (about 600 B.C.) described how she got an attack of panic "out of a clear blue sky". Julius Caesar became extremely anxious whenever he saw a cat. And Charles Darwin was always filled with anxiety when in a crowd.

Although we commonly speak of anxiety, we should make a distinction between it and fear. Fear is the reaction of the mind and body to events such as an apparently threatening noise, an electric shock, or a gun pointed at us. Anxiety, on the other hand, is an emotion caused by something imagined in the future, such as the bullet wound, and can range from a diffuse feeling to a mood of impending disaster.

In anxiety the stimulus producing fear is either not present or is not immediately threatening; it is imagined or anticipated, leading to mental and physical arousal. But the arousal, vigilance, physiological preparedness, negative emotions and cognitions occur in both and the symptoms of anxiety and fear are very similar. A vast number of internal or external factors can trigger off the anxiety symptoms of panic, agoraphobia, post-traumatic stress disorder, specific phobias, and generalized anxiety disorder.

Both fear and anxiety are stored in the depths of the brain, and throughout the millions of years of evolution these complex biological and neurophysiological programs have proved to be exceptionally useful, enabling us to either counter or avoid danger ("fight or flight").

Is anxiety in our genes?

To be afraid of such things as poisonous snakes or spiders, heights or strangers, was evolved as a survival strategy and became an instinct in most people from childhood on. The degree of anxiety, however, is different from person to person. There are worlds between Ernest Hemingway, who welcomed risk and was at the same time self-destructive, and Franz Kafka, the Austrian writer ("The Trial", etc.) who was continually anxious for his life. It is very probable that genetic make-up plays a significant role here, and the attention of experts is directed nowadays to this rather than to bad experiences in childhood. Is the disposition to anxiety inherited, like diabetes for example?

Research with rats and mice, in which over 90% of the genes which have a role in sickness are in common with our own, has shown by breeding both "anxious" and "courageous" mice that this is indeed the case. But the research goes further. If the newborn of an anxious mother is "adopted" by a courageous mother this has hardly any effect on its later behavior. According to this the genes are stronger than the upbringing. But other research shows that upbringing does have an effect and the current opinion is that 50% of anxiety disorders are genetic in origin and 50% due to upbringing. If there is a genetic disposition to anxiety in the family and at least one parent is overprotective of a child, then its tendency to anxiety will be increased. In addition, unpleasant experiences or excessive demands on the child can cause the anxiety genes to assert themselves. But after all, mice are not men! It is probably correct that we inherit the disposition to anxiety but not the anxiety itself.

Question: Do you think your early experiences were at least partly the source of your anxiety?

It's quite normal to be anxious

Anxiety, worry and fear can be very normal. You become anxious when threatened or even when you think about being threatened. The heart beats faster, there is a need to breathe harder, you get the cold sweats and shakes. These are all normal changes that step up physical performance if we have to run or fight; survival reactions inherited from our earliest ancestors. But nowadays we are often threatened by situations where physical activity is both unnecessary and counter-productive. The bodily changes still take place and we see them as harmful and unnatural – we can actually worry and get anxious about them, for instance about sweating when having an interview.

Being a little anxious is a valuable ability. It sharpens up judgment and skill so that we can cope better. Being psyched up is a good thing if you have a difficult challenge ahead. Anxiety and stress arouse us, enabling us to meet a threat or challenge and spurs us to appropriate action, gearing us up to face a threatening situation. They make you study harder for that exam, and keep you on your toes when you're making a speech. The tension you get when the boss is angry helps you stand up to him, ready to defend yourself. A little anxiety before an examination or interview is stimulating, but too much may lead to failure. The problem is that anxiety may go too far.

If anything can possibly go wrong... it will!

So says Murphy's Law and there has always been plenty to be anxious about; fear of losing your job, of not having enough food or money or what your neighbors or the public think about you, or not being a success, fear of pain, disease and death, anxiety about losing your loved ones. There is the fear of flying, of driving, of heights, of being in closed or alternatively open spaces. And there is the general anxiety that *something* will go wrong. Perhaps the worst thing about that is that it can be a self-fulfilling prophecy.

You are not to blame

Unlike mice, we humans are not completely programmed by our genes but process the information we received through our senses according to our past experiences. We can think far into the future to make optimistic plans or produce horrific scenarios – these can become powerful sources of anxiety. Many anxiety patients acquire a processing strategy in which they habitually interpret events or sensations such as a throbbing heart as dangerous. They seek to avoid whatever caused the anxiety. This creates a vicious circle in which the anxiety threshold becomes lower and lower. "What will happen? It doesn't bear thinking about!" Exactly, because when we brood over it, we become liable to anxiety attacks and panic.

Anxiety disorders are not signs of a character flaw, nor is it likely that we are born anxious. Probably the simplest explanation is the best; that the emotions get out of control like a diabetic's blood sugar level or a heart patient's blood pressure. Chronic or extreme anxiety and phobias are the result of thought processes which give rise to negative emotions. Once you realize and accept this you are in a better position to heal them.

Stress is a powerful factor for anxiety, though the steps from daily stress and spontaneous anxiety to an actual anxiety disorder blur into one another. The fright of a near collision on the highway is like a panic attack, which can recur at any time as if out of nowhere. Surveys show that nearly all people have worries. They are afraid of unemployment, separation, are anxious about their families and above all of severe illness. Almost every second person has anxiety about cancer, women more than men. These "everyday" anxieties can lead to sleep problems, irritability, headaches and stomach ache, particularly when stress is also involved. There can be vicious circles here; being anxious about whether you will be anxious leads to sleepless nights.

As we saw, normal anxiety is essential, increasing the level of adrenaline in the blood, enabling increased performance, faster reactions and sharpness of the senses. Every manager and sportsman knows this feeling. But it can also lead to a "crash" if anxiousness about being anxious becomes too great. When this happens, students facing their exams can't sleep, and even the toughest managers can fall into a chaos of emotions when faced with doing a major presentation or when they have exaggerated expectations of their own success but this is followed by failure.

Specific anxieties and what they can lead to

Almost any event in life can lead to a low level anxiety which can spread to almost any problem – might your credit cards be stolen? – and this kind of anxiety, if not checked, can lead to what is medically known as the General Anxiety Disorder, and which we will in the next chapter also call excessive worrying. It is a general apprehensiveness based on Murphy's Law. It does not mean that everyone who is sometimes a bit apprehensive needs therapy, but it can lead to more serious anxiety disorders. Specific anxieties can lead to panic, phobias or obsessions, which we will come to in later chapters.

How anxiety actually does lead to a more serious, possibly chronic disorder, is not clear, but continuing stress increases the risk. The situation becomes serious when anxiety and panic occur without any apparent reason. When they do, a visit to a therapist is advisable, but don't be put off with "anxiety" pills, which do not solve the problem.

All psychologists agree that anxiety disorders are widespread. The Inuit (Eskimos) mention kayak anxiety, which disorients them and gives the feeling of falling into nowhere. "Koro" is the belief amongst Malaysians and Chinese that the penis will withdraw into the body and kill its "owner". In Singapore in 1967 there was a panic after the press reported that there were cases of koro after eating pork. Only with considerable difficulty could the Health Ministry convince men that the idea of a shrinking genital was merely the result of anxiety.

Keeping our anxiety under control will certainly not end the reasons for it, but it will allow us to think calmly and rationally about them and be able to take the best possible action to defend ourselves, our families, friends and, indeed, the nation and all humanity. But if you have an anxiety disorder, this normally helpful emotion can do just the opposite – it can keep you from coping and can disrupt your daily life.

Question: We are all afraid of something, and we are anxious that it might happen. Do you know your own fears?

Accepting anxiety

Acceptance is not approval of what is happening but the essential process of telling yourself the truth about your present reality. It is one of the most important skills we need to cope with an anxiety disorder. It is a skill that functions at various levels. To find out whether you are on the anxiety danger list there is a questionnaire in the next chapter with which you can check what applies to you.

The first level of acceptance concerns the physical symptoms of anxiety. You may react to these as unbearable, terrible and even dangerous. If for example you regard palpitations as dangerous, you are likely to become anxious about having a heart attack, and in extreme cases the stress of this can actually cause one. An anxious person, however, can learn to raise their tolerance of the symptoms and so not be obsessed by these bodily sensations. This is accomplished by changing your interpretation of the sensations. What you are doing is changing "awful, terrible things" into merely "uncomfortable feelings".

Put the book down for a while (or watch the screen saver) and think this over. How does it apply to you?

The next level of acceptance requires learning to approve of oneself in a very realistic way. If you are a person with anxiety, it does no good to berate yourself over this fact. Anxiety is nothing to be ashamed of or to feel guilty about since we do not have direct control over our emotions. You do not have to keep it secret or hide it from the world. Anxiety just seems to come from nowhere and if you persistently remind yourself that it just happens, like the weather, you can truly admit to yourself and to others (at the right times) that you are a highly sensitive person who can be over-anxious. That's well within normality.

The final level of acceptance comes from progress in accepting the discomfort of physical symptoms and of your "anxious self". It will happen when you no longer care much if you feel anxiety because you have gained the confidence that any anxiety you feel will stay within a tolerable range. You will reach this deep level of acceptance once you have mastered the skills of proper breathing, relaxation, countering unrealistic thoughts, and practiced graduated exposure in facing your fears. At this stage you will no longer be concerned about feeling symptoms of anxiety, but simply do whatever you choose to do, as if you had no anxiety. The paradox of this type of deep acceptance is that you accept the symptoms of anxiety, freeing yourself of the restrictions you used to impose on yourself. You can ask yourself if you would do a certain thing if you did not have anxiety. If the answer is "yes", you can go ahead and do it. This is the ultimate acceptance and frees you from any bonds that your anxiety disorder placed on you.

Exercises for specific anxieties

Although the ideal is to do the exercises every day, it is adequate if you have two sessions a week. Allow an hour each time.

Begin each session with a breathing exercise (Chapter 6). This will calm you down. Then do ONE of the exercises given below, starting with Exercise 1. Do the exercise for at least a week, then do the next one for another week, and then decide which suits you best and continue with it. End each session with some of the Breathing and Movement exercises, which will make you more aware of yourself.

Read through the whole description of each exercise before you do it.

NOTE: If at any time during these exercises your feelings get too strong, stop.

Exercise 1. The "What would happen if...?" game

You are anxious about your job, marriage, finances, etc, so you play the game, "If I did this or that..." But then you remember that your thoughts are just thoughts, but not reality. Several possibilities of what might happen come up in your imagination, but you can't decide which will really be best. At least you can reflect calmly on them, which will help you to make a rational rather than an emotional decision. Perhaps you can relax better if you stay for a time with whichever outcome would make you happiest.

If you have a strong anxiety it is very likely that you

will become fixated on only one possible outcome, usually the worst possible, and this will become your present reality. "I HAVE got cancer" instead of "Let's wait for the examination results". The game allows your imagination to open up the possibility of other, less worrying outcomes.

Exercise 2. Putting the anxiety on video tape

Before and after the visualization exercise which follows, do breathing or mindfulness exercises to relax you (Chapters 6 and 7).

Sit down comfortably and relax, then close your eyes. Visualize a TV in front of you and its remote control in your hand. The set has a video recorder, so put an empty cassette in it. Switch the TV on. The screen is blank but the video will record anything that comes on it.

Think about the feared result of whatever your anxiety is about – the cancer examination for example. Your anxiety may go a stage further and you may actually "experience" lying in hospital waiting for the operation. If your anxiety is about your marriage, you may feel you are already in the lawyer's office... or...

Each of these experiences has a certain color and shape. What are they? Put them on the TV screen; they will be automatically recorded. Now switch the TV and video off. Take the cassette out.

Finally visualize a safe, big enough to walk in. Go inside and put the cassette on an empty shelf, far back. Come out of the safe and close the door. Lock it with the key, which you keep in a safe place.

Exercise 3. Viewing your anxieties

In your next session, get the key to the safe, unlock it, take the cassette out and put it in the video. Now play it so that you see the color and shape of your anxiety again. Watch the picture for a while. Now look, not at the picture itself, but at its edge. After a while the picture will get smaller and smaller until it is just a tiny rectangle in the middle of the screen. After you have done this a few times the anxiety will fade away completely; you can no longer see it and the cassette is empty. If you have several anxieties, do them one at a time. You will be facing up to and accepting your anxiety.

How the exercise works

By looking at your anxiety while relaxed, you don't get the symptoms of sweating, trembling and so on because these exercises create a distance between you and the anxiety, bringing it under control. This works well with people who have a strong power of imagination, but it also helps those who are rather "rational" beings if they practice it over a number of sessions.

Chapter 3

DON'T WORRY – BE HAPPY!

The worst possible advice that chronic worriers can be given is to stop worrying. It's like telling someone with a cold not to have a runny nose. Bouts of worrying come unasked, and once they start they are likely to persist. But fortunately there are ways in which they can be brought under control.

There is a difference between anxiety and fear. Fear is an emotional state which arises when something definite or a real threat is there to cause it. People with asthma are fearful or even terrified when they find that they suddenly can't breathe, and that makes the attack worse. Being attacked or being told you have a tumor are other examples. Under such circumstances, fearful thoughts or experiences come into the mind and these often lead to panic, desperation and the feeling of total loss of control. This is a very dangerous reaction, because it makes you incapable and irrational just when you need to keep a cool head and a clear mind.

General anxiety is a strongly reactive state of emotion, but the cause or threat often cannot be clearly identified. It is a general state of insecurity and jumpiness that can be started by almost anything or by nothing you are aware of, so that you feel anxious and have no idea why. You may wake up feeing tense and anxious and even if you are aware of a cause, the anxiety you feel is frequently out of all proportion to it. You may be worrying all the time and have the feeling that, "If it's not one darn thing it's another" – Murphy's Law again. This state of mind can become a chronic condition.

Generalized anxiety

Chronic worry, "Generalized Anxiety Disorder" as it is known, is a relatively common problem that turns daily life into a state of worry, anxiety, and fear. It is characterized by excessive thinking and dwelling on the "what ifs". As a result, you feel there's no way out of the vicious cycle of anxiety and worry, and then you become depressed about life and the state you find yourself in.

Generalized anxiety usually does not cause people to avoid situations in which they might feel anxious (like phobias) and there isn't an element of a "panic attack" involved either. It is the continual anxious thinking, dwelling on worries and ruminating on them, and the inability to shut these off, that so incapacitates you. At times other thoughts may be almost non-existent because the anxious feelings are so dominant. Feelings of worry, dread, lack of energy, and a loss of interest in life are common. Many times there is no "basis" or "cause" for these feelings and you should try to realize that they are irrational. Nevertheless, the feelings are very real and they drain away all energy and zest for life.

It gets worse. You are irritated or even angry with yourself for being so irrational!

Test yourself for general anxiety disorder (chronic anxiety)

In the following list, check the points which apply to you:

1 Have you for six months or longer been continually anxious, tense and worried?

2 Do you worry over things which are in reality unlikely to happen?

3 Do you frequently worry about things which are not so difficult after all?

4   Do you have worries in several areas, e.g. children, work, family, health?

5   At the times when you feel anxious and worried:
- do you get tired easily?
- are you excited, nervous or jumpy?
- do you quiver or shake?
- do you feel restless and uneasy?
- do your muscles get tense or painful?
- have you severe problems of concentration?
- are you easily excitable?
- do you perspire a great deal?
- does your heart thump or race?
- are your hands cold and moist?
- do you feel dizzy or dazed?
- do you have a dry mouth?
- do you feel sick or have diarrhea?
- do you need to pass water frequently?
- do you feel hot or have the cold shivers?
- are you breathless or do you have a choking feeling?
- is swallowing a problem?
- do you keep waking up at night?
- do you feel close to fainting or have a feeling of unreality?
- do you feel you might lose control?

Assessing your anxiety test

If you have checked questions 1 and 4 or several items in question 5 you are probably suffering from the General Anxiety Disorder, in which anxiety is a chronic condition and can spread to almost any area of your life. If you feel you have a GAD, do the Program for three months. If during that time things get worse or at the end you are not better, consult a therapist, as you may need medication.

Forms of anxiety and worry

Anxiety comes in two forms, *cognitive*, which means conscious thoughts and *somatic*, meaning the physiological symptoms which were listed in the questionnaire. To become aware of these is usually the best way to diagnose your anxiety. You may then become anxious about them, but at least you begin to know their cause.

When concerned with a particular problem or threat, worry is not harmful but may actually be constructive. The anxiety forces attention on the problem, and the mind is concentrated on how to handle it and ignores anything else for the time being. In a sense this is a rehearsal of what might go wrong and how to deal with it. The task of this kind of worrying is to find positive solutions for life's risks and dangers by anticipating them before they arise. However this does not always work well. New solutions and fresh ways of seeing do not come from continual worry, for the worrier may simply fixate on the danger itself and become trapped in his fear.

Chronic repetitive worries – the film again

> *Oh, no! The muffler sounds bad... What if I have to take it to the shop? ... I can't afford the expense... I'd have to draw the money from Jamie's college fund... What if I can't afford his tuition? ... That bad school report last week... What if his grades go down and he can't get into college... Muffler sounds bad...*
>
> "The Work of Worrying" by L Roemer and T Borkovec in Handbook of Mental Control, Wegner and Pennebaker.

The difficulty with chronic repetitive worrying is that it goes on and on without getting any nearer to a positive solution. The worries come from nowhere and are uncontrollable. They produce a continuous background of anxious feeling, are not amenable to reason and lock the worrier into a single, inflexible view of the worrisome situations.

The emotions of fear and worry can be very strong. If a loved one is ten minutes late, the person with repetitive anxiety fears the very worst – "Something's dreadfully wrong. After all, he's ten minutes late!

There's been an accident, the paramedics are taking him to the hospital and his injuries are just too critical to resuscitate him... Oh, my God! WHAT AM I GOING TO DO?" Feelings of fear and anxiety rush in from these thoughts, and the vicious cycle of anxiety and depression runs wild.

The film of chronic anxiety

You will remember from Chapter 1 that anxious people often "make a film" of the future events about which they are anxious and run it over and over again. This is particularly true of generalized anxiety disorder. The film is an endless loop, but the director keeps introducing new scenes and the old ones might be forgotten, then remembered again.

The film in the mind projects its various worries in an endless loop. The effect intensifies and persists and may easily shade over into full-blown disorders: phobias, attacks of panic, obsessions and compulsions (such as very frequent hand-washing for fear of germs and dirt). When that happens the anxieties focus on particular situations or happenings, a disaster for example, and, in the case of panic, the prospect of having the next attack.

Exercise 4. "Stopping the film" – first session

Read the description of each exercise completely before you start it.

Although the ideal is to do the exercises every day, it is adequate if you have two sessions a week. Allow at least an hour each time.

Begin each session with a breathing exercise (Chapter 7). This will calm you down. Then do ONE of the exercises given below. Do that exercise for at least a week, then do the other, decide which suits you best and continue with it. End each session with some of the Breathing and Movement exercises, which will make you more aware of yourself.

Sit down as relaxed as possible. The best place is the chair or couch where you normally watch TV, but of course don't switch it on. Close your eyes. You visualize the inner TV and have the remote control in your hand so you can choose the program you want. A video with an empty cassette is connected to the inner TV and will record everything that comes on the screen.

Be sure there is a "still" or "pause" button on the remote control and that it works. Now choose one of the things you are anxious about, put a possibly even frightening scene from it on the screen, and press the "still" button. Keep looking at it, *but if your anxiety gets too strong break off and do either a breathing exercise (Chapter 6) or "Calm and Distance" (Chapter 7).*

When you feel calmer, start the film again choosing a different anxiety and look at it for a while after pressing the still button. Remember that you can break off any time things get too much for you.

Now look, not at the picture itself, but at a point on the edge of the frame. After a while, shrink the picture until it is just a tiny square in the middle. All this has been recorded, but now switch the TV and video off. Take the cassette out.

In the same way you can record and shrink each of your major anxieties. Now put the cassette away in the safe as in the exercise "Putting the anxiety on tape".

Exercise 5."Stopping the film" – second and further sessions

At the start of the next session take the cassette from the safe and play the anxieties one by one. Start with one that gives you moderate but not excessive feelings. Now do the following exercise while keeping the anxiety on the screen.

NOTE: If you have asthma, heart problems or psychic illness do not do the following breathing exercise. Instead simply sit relaxed or do Body Scan (Chapter 7).

Breathe in deeply and then stretch out the out-breath as long as you can – it could be for up to a minute. This won't have any bad effects but don't try to beat the record. So long as you keep the in-breaths short and the out-breaths long you will match your own natural rhythm of breathing and will feel calm and quiet.

Shrink the picture as you did in the first session and put the cassette away.

The whole exercise should take about 10 minutes. Depending on how you feel, go to another anxiety. *Repeat the exercise regularly.*

How the exercise works

The exercise begins with getting your breathing under control (Chapter 8). Quick and flat breathing, even panting, is an inborn reaction to excited states, as are other symptoms such as high pulse rate and blood pressure. By doing exercises that slow down your breathing, which is the easiest function to reach, the other functions will also slow down. If your heart continues to race, wait quietly and it will slow down too. If you get into a calm state for only a short time, this is already progress. With regular practice this will last longer.

What you are doing in this exercise is learning to remain relaxed when facing an anxiety. The physical symptoms of anxiety fade away and you are free to deal with the situation with clarity. And the film? Once you lose some of your anxieties, cut those out of the film so that it is no longer a loop running round and round. Instead you can deal with those that are left one by one. Perhaps you will win that Oscar after all!

The benefit of mindfulness

The most important aspect of the Anxiety Relief Program is that it is based on mindfulness, which, as we saw in Chapter 1, is moment-to-moment awareness of your thoughts and feelings without judging them as "good" or "bad". It changes your relationship to thoughts and, above all, to your feelings. Rather than saying, "I am afraid" or "I am anxious", both of which make *you part of the fear or anxiety,* with mindfulness you can say, "I have fearful thoughts", period. You no longer identify yourself with them and so have feelings about them, but are simply aware of them and accept them. This is a further stage in the acceptance we spoke of in Chapter 2. There is more about mindfulness and how to cultivate it in Chapter 6.

Chapter 4

COPING WITH PANIC

Panic is only too familiar from the news headlines. At a soccer game in England in 1989 a great many people were crushed to death when panic broke out. In a Chicago club early in 2003, 21 people were trampled to death when a fire started. Diving back into history, at the battle of Marathon in 490 B.C., although the Persian army was ten times the size of the Greek army, they panicked and ran away, leaving the Greeks victorious. Why? The Greeks thanked the god Pan for their victory; modern neurophysiologists explain that people fall into panic when they feel threatened and are afraid they cannot control the situation – they go on to explain the workings of this in the brain, but that's all Greek to us...

More important to us than the question of how panic

occurs, is how to be able to prevent it in ourselves. A remarkable fact about 9/11 was that the survivors of the attack, as they report, did not feel helpless against the danger and so did not panic. They therefore remained reasonable and were ready to give help to others, which is one of the best ways to prevent panic. Can we, as individuals, keep ourselves under control? There is a clue here.

There does not have to be a catastrophe for many people to suffer from panic attacks. These are incidents during which intense fear and discomfort are experienced *for no apparent reason*. If you suffer from such attacks you almost certainly have no idea why you get them or when they will happen; there is no warning signal and so you cannot prepare yourself to ward off an attack – at least not in the short term. There is a longer term answer in the form of breathing and mindfulness exercises, but we will come to these later.

Panic Disorder (PD) is a broad-brush label currently applied to a variety of conditions having clearly distinct origins, including:

Phobic sensitization. This means that the fear of having panic attacks actually increases the liability to further ones, which is why it is so important to bring them under control and to realize that they are not dangerous.

Prolonged stress. Under long lasting stress the

likelihood of panic attacks increases. The mindfulness exercises of the Program are also used in stress reduction programs and so have a double purpose.

Anxious or obsessive patterns of thinking. Repetitive anxieties and worries and ways to overcome them are described in Chapter 3.

Poor breathing habits, whether rooted in anxiety or other causes. The exercises in Chapter 7, when done consistently, will greatly improve your breathing habits.

These are the best known causes and, together with one or two concepts such as "false suffocation alarm" and "separation anxiety," are considered the "classic" ones. Others include a hereditary defect in the metabolism involved with regulating both digestion and stress endorphins. People with this form of PD may have escalating gastrointestinal symptoms, such as reflux disease or irritable bowel syndrome for years or decades before the emergence of panic attacks. There are further symptoms of panic mentioned in the medical literature but they are referred to as either "yet to be isolated" or "not yet identified" and so need not concern us here.

What happens if panic disorder is neglected?

PD tends to continue for months or years. It typically begins in young adulthood, but the symptoms may arise earlier or later in life. If neglected, it may worsen to the point where the person's life is seriously affected by panic attacks and by attempts to avoid or conceal them. In fact, many people have had problems with friends and family or lost jobs while struggling to cope with panic disorder. It does not usually go away by itself but gets worse unless treated.

Test yourself for panic disorder

The questionnaire below will give a guide to whether you might have a panic disorder and also acquaint you with the symptoms that arise from it. Check the points that apply to you.

1 Have you ever been suddenly and unexpectedly overcome with strong anxiety in a situation in which most people are not anxious?

2 Strong anxiety happens in situations of real danger or when you are the center of attention. But do your panic attacks come when you are *not* in such a situation?

3 Try to remember what happened in your worst panic attack.
   - Were you short of breath?
   - Did you breathe quickly or even pant?
   - Did your heart thump?
   - Were you dizzy or light-headed?
   - Did you have a tight feeling in the belly or chest?
   - Did you have tingling or numbness anywhere?
   - Did you have a choking feeling?
   - Did you feel close to fainting?
   - Did you perspire?
   - Did you shiver or shake?
   - Did you feel waves of heat or chill down the back?
   - Did you feel a need to vomit?
   - Did you have a dry mouth?
   - Did things around you seem unreal?*
   - Were you afraid of dying?*
   - Were you afraid of going crazy?*
4 Did these symptoms come very suddenly and get worse after a few minutes?

5 Have you had at least four panic attacks in a month?

6 After such an attack are you continually anxious about getting another one?*

Assessing the questionnaire

If you have checked questions 1 and 2, and at least one symptom in questions 3, 4, 5 or 6 you probably have a panic disorder. Panic disorder is present when there are both recurrent panic attacks and either a fear of having another or a fear of losing control, having a heart attack, or "going crazy". If you also avoid situations where you think you might panic you may have agoraphobia as well as panic disorder.

You will notice that the symptoms marked * are different to all the others because they are fears rather than physical sensations. One of the most frightening things about a panic attack is that you don't know what is happening to you or why. Because there doesn't seem to be any reason for these sudden and intense physical symptoms, most people interpret them to mean that they are about to lose control, have a heart attack, die or go crazy. In other words, they take the symptoms as a sign that something dangerous is happening. This interpretation is very significant because it can contribute to the cycle of panic. If you go to your doctor and he says you are *not* having a heart attack or going crazy you may be disconcerted because you feel certain that *something* is terribly wrong and the doctor has not spotted it. In emergency rooms people are usually told "nothing is wrong" and are sent home without any help or with merely a prescription for tranquilizers. But of course there are doctors who do recognize panic and will reassure you that you are not in danger.

It is reassuring to know that you are not going to die or go crazy, but far more so to know that you can end the turmoil in mind and body by becoming aware of how thoughts in your mind can form a chain reaction leading to the "explosions". For many victims of PD, thoughts, fears, and physical reactions become automatic and create a great deal of anxiety. There are proven methods for countering or neutralizing these thoughts and reactions, and these methods are the essentials of the exercises you will be doing. Retraining your breathing and knowing positively that you can prevent attacks are essential to success in your recovery from panic disorder.

Agoraphobia

Agoraphobia occurs when you are anxious about being in places or situations where you might have a panic attack. Hence you either avoid these situations, only go to such places with a companion, or you endure them but with severe anxiety. Agorophobia is named after the Agora, the public meeting place in ancient Greek cities, which was no doubt very crowded and noisy.

Most commonly, agoraphobia involves a fear of going into places where it might be difficult or embarrassing to escape quickly in case of a panic attack and you need to get away, or places where there is no quick access to medical help.

Agoraphobia sometimes develops with patients retreating to smaller and smaller "safe zones" close to home or even within limited areas of the home. It can even occur together with pre-emergent PD, becoming one of the first behavioral signs of what is to come, so that a patient who has not yet experienced panic attacks grows more and more reluctant to leave areas of familiarity and comfort.

What causes all those feelings you get during a panic attack? Like many other processes in the human body, they take place "by themselves", in fact controlled by the autonomous nervous system, so that we don't have to think about them at all, like breathing. When we exercise, the muscles in our body need more oxygen so we start to breathe more quickly, but we don't *choose* to do this, it just happens automatically.

Another important automatic process is the well-known "fight or flight response". This is an in-built safety device which allows us to respond very quickly whenever we are threatened or in danger. This response evolved in the remote past when most of the threats to our survival were physical, and it helped us to move quickly to fight off a predator or escape from the dangerous situation. You can see this happening in many animal films. When our fight or flight response is triggered adrenaline and other hormones are released into the body, causing various changes such as increasing our heart and breathing rates, and tensing our muscles ready for action. We also start to sweat and have a strong urge to flee. These reactions would be useful if we had to run or fight, but in most situations nowadays it is almost never appropriate to either run or fight. But you still react as though it was. All that extra oxygen you breathe in and the extra carbon dioxide you breathe out can start to make you feel dizzy and light-headed, even nauseous. Your arms and legs may start to shake and you may get muscle cramps from being tense for too long.

If you think these sound like the symptoms of a panic attack, you're right! A panic attack happens when your fight or flight response "goes off" and you breathe more than you need and get other symptoms, which occur because your body is trying to protect itself from danger. The symptoms do not actually harm you, but they are unnecessary and can be very unpleasant.

What sets off panic?

Panic and agarophobia are started not by "dangers" such as boarding a plane, entering a lift or driving on an unknown highway. These are not dangers at all, or at any rate only remotely. It is when we *judge* them to be immediate and real dangers that fight-or-flight takes control and we are in panic. There does not have to be a logical reason such as noticing a crack in the wing of the plane. The very thought, "What if I lose control and have a panic attack?" or remembering that you had a panic attack in the same place once before, is enough.

This happens because the thought of a panic attack is itself very scary, simply because you believe that you might not survive the next one. If this were really true you would indeed be in great danger, and so your body activates the fight or flight response.

Just as important as knowing that panic is not fatal is to realize that you can work with those mind-body storms by changing the way in which you see and judge situations, consciously or as a matter of habit. This is achieved by "mindfulness" (see Chapter 6), which makes you aware of the processes of thought and reactivity in your own mind. All the exercises in this book have the aim of increasing mindfulness in one way or another.

First aid for panic and agoraphobia

These exercises stop you from over breathing during a panic attack and calm you down.

Each exercise is a new skill, so you need to practice them in relaxed situations, at least three times a day for ten minutes each. Try out each exercise, choose the one that suits you best, and continue practicing it.

The tanden

Before beginning with the exercises you should know about the "tanden". This is a Japanese word meaning the area around a point called the "hara", three fingers' width below the navel. It is the point of physical and psychic balance. Hara breathing is what we later call belly breathing.

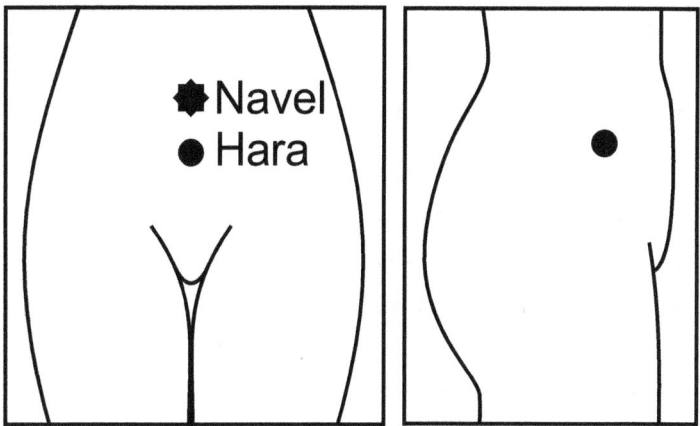

Exercise 6. Tanden-Do, the way of the belly

There are many places where you don't want to be seen obviously doing an exercise, as people might think you are acting strangely. The Japanese exercise Tanden-Do is ideal in this case. You can do it as long as you like, but once you have learned it even a minute helps. You can do it sitting at a table during a meal or a meeting, in the train, in the car or at traffic lights when your impatience mounts (this might save an accident). I have had patients who have even done it standing in line at the supermarket checkout. It didn't make the bill less, but it helped them to keep calm when the person in front was searching for their credit card.

I have also taught this exercise to patients who had anxiety or even panic attacks at the dentist's, or just at the thought of it. They first trained themselves at home with a special cassette and could then get up enough courage to make an appointment (you'd be surprised how many can't even manage that). Once in the dentist's chair they could lie back, do the exercise and let the dentist get on happily with his work.

You can do Tanden-Do sitting on a chair or sofa. Do not sit with crossed legs or slumped against the backrest, for these never bring relaxation but simply increase tension. When you slump back your spine is not straight, and if your arms are on the desk your shoulders become tense. All tensions are unnecessary activity, so be aware of your posture and correct it if necessary

At a meal or in a meeting, you can keep your hand hidden under the table, which will save you from any embarrassment.

There are two positions in which to do Tanden-Do normally, though you can also try it standing up – resting against the back of a chair or even leaning against a wall.

If there is no other way, just stand.

Lying back on the couch or in bed, place one hand, but *not both*, on your belly and feel its movement up and down, up and down... That is all you need do. Make no attempt to control your breathing and do not count your breaths; you will find that after a short while your breathing gets slower and more regular by itself. Many thoughts may come into your head, but let them pass and then return to the movement of your belly, up and down, up and down...

Tanden-Do is particularly helpful if you have difficulty in getting to sleep. Do it in your normal sleeping position.

Exercise 7. Slow breathing in six-second rhythm

The slow breathing technique stops you from over-breathing during a panic attack. It helps you to settle down, stop releasing adrenaline into your system, and turns off the "fight or flight" response.

Naturally there are many situations where you can't do this exercise. In that case do Tanden-Do, with your hand hidden under the table or desk. But normally you can do slow breathing.

- Breathe in deeply for six seconds (time it the first time).

- Hold your breath for six seconds.

- Breath fully out for six seconds.

- Hold your breath for six seconds.

- Breathe in again, and so on.

Be sure you do not speed up the rhythm. Repeat for up to 10 minutes or when your anxiety drops away.

Exercise 8. Putting your panic on tape

Before and after the visualization exercise which follows do breathing or mindfulness exercises, which will relax you (Chapters 6 and 7).

Sit down comfortably and relax, then close your eyes. Visualize a TV in front of you and its remote control in your hand. The set has a video recorder, so put an empty cassette in it. Switch the TV on. The screen is blank but the video will record anything that comes on it.

NOTE: This is a powerful exercise that may cause you some discomfort, as you may get symptoms of panic. If even the thought of panic is too distressing, do not do this exercise, but concentrate on "mindfulness" exercises (Chapter 6). If you do decide to do the exercise, do so very carefully, not going too far in each session.

What you are going to do on this exercise is to imagine a panic situation on the screen. IT IS THE "YOU" ON THE SCREEN THAT GETS INTO PANIC, NOT YOU YOURSELF. You are the viewer, not the actor. You can watch everything that happens on the screen and you have control of the situation – after all, you have a remote control.

You need not go right into the situation to begin with, but you should approach it gradually. If you are going to go up in the lift, begin at the other end of the corridor and walk slowly towards it. If you have to give a speech, you are still outside the hall or, if you are to board a plane you are waiting at the gate for the flight to be called, and so on. What does the "you" on the screen feel and think? Have "you" any panic symptoms? If the feelings get too strong, close your eyes and do Tanden-Do or six second breathing for five minutes or so. Concentrate on each breath as it happens and if any thoughts about the situation come, just breathe them out.

When you feel calmer, open your eyes. Now let the "you" on the screen get nearer to the lift, onto the stage, along the walk to the door of the plane, further along the highway or whatever it happens to be. Again, watch "your" reactions and if they get too strong, do a breathing exercise.

Gradually you get nearer to what you want to do – get into the lift, take your seat on the plane or walk on to the stage.

But you probably won't get there the first time. When you have done the exercise and hopefully made a little progress, switch off and put the tape away. Next time start where you left off. You should repeat the exercise two or three times a week until you can say, "Mission accomplished! Without panic!"

Chapter 5

PHOBIAS AND COMPULSIONS

Fear is a very ancient and universal emotion in man. It is the feeling that you are in immediate danger, that something bad is about to happen, and it is almost always accompanied by a host of often disturbing physical symptoms which we have seen in Chapter 2. The first questions to ask yourself *after* you have read this chapter through (please!) are,

- "Do I suffer from at least some of these physical symptoms when fear is not justified by a real danger or threat, or by any rational cause?" And,

- "Does my fear lead me to avoidance of the situations in which I feel likely to get it?"

If you answer both these questions with "yes", you

may have what is called a phobia, which is actually a kind of panic reaction caused by specific stimuli or situations. Phobias are the most common form of anxiety disorder. A study by the National Institute of Mental Health found phobias were the most common psychiatric illness among women in all age groups and the second most common illness among men older than 25. Some anxiety disorders, like panic disorder, appear to have a stronger genetic basis than others, although the actual genes concerned have yet not been identified. Other anxiety disorders are more rooted in stressful life events.

If you look at the lists of phobias compiled by many psychologists, you will be amazed at how there is almost nothing from A to Z – aerophobia (fear of air) to zoophobia (fear of animals) – that people cannot develop phobias about. The "top ten" are:

1. Arachnophobia – Fear of spiders.

2. Anthrophobia – Fear of people or society.

3. Aerophobia – Fear of drafts, breathing in noxious substances in the air.

4. Agoraphobia – Fear of being outdoors, of crowds or uncontrolled social conditions.

5. Claustrophobia – Fear of confined spaces.

6. Acrophobia – Fear of heights.

7. Cancerophobia – Fear of cancer.

8. Astraphobia – Fear of thunder and lightning.

9. Necrophobia – Fear of death or dead things.

10. Cardiophobia – Fear of heart disease.

Some fears are popularly called phobias but are really symptoms of other psychic problems, or just plain hatred. Examples are:

- Xenophobia, fear of strangers or the unknown.

- Homophobia, fear of homosexuals.

- Hydrophobia, or fear of water, is usually not a psychological condition at all, but another term for the disease rabies, although to fear the sea, lakes or rivers is quite common.

Three broad classes of phobia are generally recognized:

Agoraphobia. This is the fear of places or situations which it may be difficult to escape from without embarrassment or where medical help might not be available in case of need. This kind of fear can include going out of our own home, traveling without company, or being in the middle of a crowd, standing in queues such as a supermarket check-out, etc.

Most individuals with agoraphobia have a history of panic disorder. There is also some evidence that agoraphobia may run in families – a child who suffers separation anxiety (anxiety about being away from home and immediate family) may be predisposed to developing agoraphobia.

Social anxiety is a marked and persistent fear of particular or general social situations where there is anxiety of misbehaving in front of other people, the fear of participating in groups of any kind, of starting a conversation with strangers, of initiating a romantic encounter, of talking to persons of authority, etc.

Although social anxiety is very real to those who suffer from it, it needs to be said that "social phobia" is one of those illnesses which pharmaceutical firms have exaggerated or simply thought up to increase the sales of their "remedies", a particular case of this marketing strategy being reported in the prestigious "British Medical Journal".

The symptoms of social anxiety include:

- Intense anxiety that you will do or say something that disgraces you in front of other people.

- Always being afraid of being watched and judged

by others, and of making mistakes.

- Avoiding doing things you want to or speaking to people because you are afraid of being embarrassed.

- Worrying for days or weeks before you have to meet new people.

- Blushing, sweating a lot, trembling, nausea, or feeling like you have to throw up before and during an event where you are with new people.

- Staying away from social situations such as parties and school events and refusing to make speeches or address meetings.

- Drinking alcohol to make your fears go away.

People who have social anxieties usually know that their fears don't make sense. But, even if they manage to face what they fear, they can still feel very uncomfortable.

Specific phobias are marked and persistent fears of certain objects and situations. Even the thought of the feared object or event can lead to a panic attack. Some of the more common specific phobias involve fear of closed-in places, heights, escalators, elevators, tunnels, injections, highway driving, bridges, water, flying, dogs, and injuries involving blood. Specific phobias often make no sense. For instance, you may be able to parachute from airplanes with ease but not be able to go above the 4th floor of an office building. Most people with these phobias know that they don't make sense. But facing their fear or even thinking about it can bring on a panic or severe anxiety attack.

Specific phobias usually start in childhood and are resolved by adulthood. Phobias caused by traumatic events, however, can occur at any age. Those beginning in adults or that continue from childhood into adulthood tend to become chronic. But many specific phobias can be "lived with" if they don't normally impair the person's ability to function in the daily routine.

The origins of phobias

Six out of every ten people who suffer phobias are able to remember when the fear crisis occurred for the first time, that is, when the sensation of panic became attached to the place or situation where it first happened. For these people there is a very clear connection between the object and the sensation of fear. For example, a man, for some unexplained reason, has a strong attack of anxiety or panic when driving. From that day on he avoids driving alone out of anxiety that he will get the same sensations again and then lose control, without anyone near him to help him.

Phobias like this may expand to other situations. In this way agoraphobia becomes an anxiety, such as an anxiety of "getting ill" and not being able to get help, or some other anxiety. The situation may then become one of general anxiety disorder.

We are what we think! Or are we?

A famous Roman philosopher, Epitites, said it is not the things of this world that hurt us but what we think about them. The way we think when we have a phobia can perpetuate it. Many people misunderstand these disorders and think one should be able to overcome the symptoms by sheer willpower. But a phobia or its symptoms can't be willed or wished away.

Regardless of the nature of your anxiety disorder your thoughts about it are very important, in particular with panic disorder and phobia. If you look at what these thoughts actually are, you will find they are catastrophic misinterpretations of bodily sensations. Now, once you learn to misinterpret these sensations, the pattern tends to be fairly enduring. So we need to become aware of such misinterpretations of the body's symptoms of anxiety and correct them. We also need to recognize that our thoughts are only thoughts which come and go but that *they are not what we actually are*. With mindfulness we can see this clearly.

How mindfulness ends phobias

Mindfulness, moment-to-moment awareness of our thoughts and feelings as they actually occur, makes us aware of our thinking patterns and emotions as well as our bodily sensations and assists us to see the damage our thoughts can cause. The way is then open for change to a more favorable pattern of thoughts.

Not only do our thoughts change but also our relationship to them. By paying attention to the process of thinking we will also see that perhaps we should change the way we think and speak about our thoughts and feelings. Rather than saying "I am afraid" or "I am anxious", both of which *make "I" into the anxiety or fear*, it would be more accurate to say, "I am having a lot of fear-filled thoughts". This emphasizes that *you are not the content of your thoughts* and do not have to identify yourself with them. Instead you can just be aware of, listen to and accept them. Then your thoughts will no longer drive you to even more fear and panic, so increasing your phobia. Instead, listening to or "watching" your thoughts can help you see more clearly what is actually on your mind and so helps you to assess the evidence which supports or does not support your beliefs about what is happening.

Is this hard to understand, seeming a bit too theoretical? Don't worry! As you practice the exercises you will experience and understand mindfulness.

Exercises for phobia

The Anxiety Relief Program uses very much the same principles as Cognitive Behavioral Therapy, one of the most successful ways of treating anxiety disorder, except that you rely on your own efforts and so are not dependent on a therapist, and you follow your own program and can exactly tailor it to your needs.

CBT is frequently accompanied by medication. The ARP is not, so that there is no risk of either physical or psychological dependence. If you feel you need medication, consult a therapist or doctor. But remember that the ideal is to do without. If you are already taking it, reduce the dose only on the advice of a doctor.

Each exercise should be done in a session lasting up to two hours, once a week at least. You cannot expect to overcome your phobia in less time. If you can't manage this much time, go to a therapist – once a week for 55 minutes is usual. Of course, such short sessions mean therapy will extend over a long period. Also, if you simply can't face working alone, consult a therapist.

Each session should look like this:

Relaxing and calming the emotions

Many people feel they can't relax and have never been able to. Part of the reason is that they are too frightened to let go of their need to be in control. Or as people do begin to relax they become fearful of the sensations in their body as it relaxes. The techniques used in the ARP are specifically selected for people with an anxiety disorder and assist them in being able to learn to let go of the control and to learn to accept the sensations of their body relaxing without fear.

Phobias are highly charged with emotions and while your brain is swirling with them you cannot expect to be able to work with them. The more your brain is quiet and relaxed, the easier the insights of mindfulness can get into it. The focus is on peace and calmness here, but not on the fear itself. Why? As peace and calmness become a little stronger, the anxieties and fears gradually fade away. Therefore, we never need to focus on the anxiety, the nervousness or the fear. Our focus is on healing, and inner peace.

The most effective techniques are:

- Slow walking (Exercise 11, Chapter 7)

- Tanden-Do (Exercise 6, Chapter 4)

- Slow breathing (Exercise 7, Chapter 4)

- Other breathing exercises (Exercises 13-15, Chapter 8)

Try these out until you discover which bring you calm

and relaxation. It can be more than one. Once you know this you should begin each session with them as a routine.

Exercise 9. Putting your phobia on tape

This exercise is similar to the ones in Chapters 3 and 4, but there are important differences, so *be sure to read the instructions through before you start.*

NOTE: This is a powerful exercise that may cause some discomfort, as symptoms of the phobia may appear. If even the thought of the phobic situation is too distressing, do not do this exercise, but concentrate on mindfulness (Chapter 6) and breathing exercises. If you do decide to do the exercise, do so very carefully, not going too far in each session. If at any time you feel panicky, anxious, or that it is just too much for you, STOP and do some of the relaxation exercises above. If you then feel better you can carry on where you left off. If you don't feel better do some Breathing and Movement exercises in Chapter 7, then go for a walk.

Sit down comfortably and relax, then close your eyes. Visualize a TV in front of you and its remote control in your hand. The set has a video recorder, so put an empty cassette in it. Switch the TV on. The screen is blank.

What you are going to do in this exercise is to imagine

the phobic situation on the screen. IT IS THE "YOU" ON THE SCREEN THAT GETS THE PHOBIA, NOT YOU YOURSELF. Everything that happens will be recorded on tape.

You are the viewer. Begin by putting the situation, including yourself, in a very small rectangle at the center of the screen. Now you can watch your thoughts and anxiety without being dominated by them. You can also watch your bodily symptoms, sweating, trembling, blushing etc, etc. You can watch everything that happens on the screen and you have control of your situation. Stay like this for a while until you begin to understand what the thoughts are that caused your fear. You might for example feel that you are standing on a platform at the top of a high building and that it is dangerous. Well, is it really, with that high railing? Or, another example, will that spider bite you or is it a harmless creature? Again, you have driven this car thousands of miles without feeling panic. Has anything changed?

When you have begun to see the phobia as the product of your thoughts, try making the picture a bit larger. Now what happens? If the phobia gets stronger, stop and do your relaxation exercise again. Then, if you can, make the picture still bigger, but if you can't do that, stop. Everything has been taped, so switch off and put the cassette away in a safe place until next time, when you can start where you left off.

Harmonizing body and mind (Exercises 13 - 18, Chapter 7)

Up to now you have been working with what is, or has been, going on in your mind. But you should not end this session without letting your mindfulness make you aware of your body as well, so bringing your whole person into harmony.

Even if time is running a bit short you should not skip this part of the session. It will relax you and help in firming up the insights into what happens when you have a phobic attack.

The exercises you should do for this are the Breathing and Movement ones in Chapter 7. Do these very slowly, so that you are aware of your breath, the feelings in your body (including how your clothes touch you) and of the thoughts coming and going in your head.

Obsessive compulsive disorder (OCD)

Obsessive-compulsive disorder (OCD) has been described as hiccups of the mind. It is a medical illness recognized by experts throughout the world, and even though some people may think those with OCD are acting peculiarly, they are not "crazy", although they may sometimes feel that way because they are troubled by thoughts and actions that they know are inappropriate. People with OCD often believe they are the only ones who have irrational, obsessive thoughts, and are therefore often ashamed and afraid to tell anyone or to seek help. But actually OCD is the fourth most common mental illness in the United States and affects approximately 5 million people. It is a potentially disabling condition that can persist throughout a person's life and if severe and untreated it can destroy their capacity to function at work, at school, or even in the home. It is treatable with considerable success both by therapy and medication and in most cases the ARP can overcome it.

Do you suffer from OCD?

A simple questionnaire will establish whether you might perhaps be an OCD sufferer. But first, we need to know exactly what is meant by obsessions and compulsions.

Obsessions are unwanted, recurrent, and disturbing thoughts, ideas and images that the person cannot suppress and which can cause overwhelming anxiety. Compulsions are repetitive, ritualized behaviors that the person feels driven to perform to alleviate the anxiety of the obsessions. The obsessive and compulsive rituals can occupy many hours of each day.

The typical cycle in a person suffering from OCD is that his obsession creates anxiety, which causes him to engage in certain actions in an attempt to alleviate the distress the obsessions cause. But carrying out these compulsive, ritual acts does not result in any permanent change and in fact makes the anxieties worse. The pattern of repetitive, senseless and distressing thoughts and behaviors can be extremely difficult to overcome. Typical examples of the OCD cycle are: "My hands may be contaminated – I must wash them" or "I may have left the gas on – I must make sure again I turned it off" or "I am going to hurt my child – I must watch myself". The cycle can, and often does, repeat itself many times over.

Please give some thought to these two questions:

Question One

Are you bothered by unpleasant thoughts which repeat themselves? Examples are:

- Being contaminated by dirt, germs, chemical, radiation, AIDS or other disease.

- Feeling that things such as the kitchen, clothing, books or tools are not perfectly arranged in order and so you must put them right – again and again.

- Thoughts of serious illness or death.

- Sexual thoughts which you cannot accept.

- Disasters such as fire, burglary, floods, earthquake or lightning happening to you.

- Financial ruin.

- A car accident.

- Losing something valuable.

- Harming a loved one through carelessness or by accident.

- Worrying about having impulses to harm yourself or someone else, steering into oncoming traffic, having inappropriate sex, etc.

- Checking light switches, locks, the cooker, faucets, etc. repeatedly.

- Counting, arranging or evening up things (like socks you are wearing being at the same height).

- Repeating actions such as sitting down, going through a door, stirring your coffee until it feels "just right".

- Touching things or people.

- Checking something you have written over and over.

- Reading everything you see in the house or outside.

- Examining yourself for signs of illness more frequently than is normal.

- Repeatedly asking to be reassured that you acted or said something correctly.

Question Two

Do you feel driven to perform certain acts over and over again? Examples are: Washing, cleaning or grooming yourself as a ritual.

If your answer to Question One is "yes" but you say "no" to Question Two, you are not suffering from OCD but you have strong anxieties which you should deal with using the exercise "Putting the anxiety on tape" in Chapter 2.

If you answer "yes" to both questions you may have OCD severely from time to time, though there may be long intervals when the symptoms are mild. But for most individuals with OCD, the symptoms are chronic and recur.

To get an idea how severe, consider your recent experience. Estimate on a scale of 0 to 4 each of the following points (it will be helpful to note your scores down):

- Time occupied by unpleasant thoughts and compulsive behaviors daily.

- How much do they distress you?

- How hard is it to control them?

- How much do they cause you to avoid situations (such as driving, cooking, etc.)?

- How much do they interfere with your life?

If you score more than a total of 5 you may well be suffering from OCD. If you score 15 or over you may require medication in addition to the ARP, in which case you should consult a therapist.

Stopping the vicious circle of OCD

We said that OCD is a cycle of obsessive anxiety and compulsion. Actually it is more revealing to say that it is a vicious circle.

An anxiety which has become an obsession causes compulsive behavior which is an effort to alleviate the anxiety. But the behavior never works and so the compulsive behavior causes anxiety that what you are doing because of it is somehow "not right" and above all unreasonable.

Anxiety, then, is the motor of OCD, which *cannot be*

overcome by attempting to control the compulsive behavior directly. Advice such as "give up washing your hands" is sometimes given, but even genuine efforts to do this result only in frustration that creates a conflict in the mind. "I want to stop, but I can't, because if I do I will be even more anxious".

Tackling the anxiety itself is therefore the way out of an OCD. Here you should go back to Chapter 2 and do the exercises in it after you have read the whole chapter. The session should always begin with relaxation, doing the following exercises in Chapter 4:

Exercise 6. Tanden-Do, the way of the belly, and

Exercise 7. Slow breathing in six second rhythm.

When you feel sufficiently calm and relaxed, do the three exercises in Chapter 2:

Exercise 1. The "What would happen if…?" game.

Here, ask yourself first if the anxiety is really justified. "Have I really contaminated my hands?" "Do I really think I might kill my partner?" And then, are these anxieties reasonable and justified? "What would happen if I didn't wash my hands?" "If I really lost my temper, would I kill her, when, after all, I've never done anything like that – I'm just not that kind of person?"

Exercise 2. Putting your anxiety on tape.

This is another TV exercise, which is described in Chapter 4 and also for reference in Chapter 7.

Exercise 3. Viewing your anxiety.

This final TV exercise should be done at the start of your next session (after relaxing). It is an opportunity to think rationally about the anxiety with which you are obsessed.

Finally, end your session with ten minutes or so of the Breathing and Movement exercises 13-18 in Chapter 6.

It is hardly likely that you will overcome OCD in just one session. But persevere and you will find it is progressively weaker and eventually at an end. If not, consult a therapist who will be able to give you medication as a support to your own efforts.

Chapter 6

WORKING WITH MINDFULNESS

You have already read quite a lot about mindfulness in this book, but one of the most important things about it is that it is NOTHING SPECIAL; as the Japanese Zen masters say, "it is just your ordinary everyday mind". It is in no way a trance, dream or ecstatic state, but just BEING FULLY AWAKE.

If it's as simple as that, why do we need to practice it? The answer is that we are not very often fully awake, but are on "automatic pilot" much of the time. How often have you driven a stretch of highway and suddenly realized you haven't noticed a thing for the last ten miles? How often have you talked to your child about a problem without being aware of your rising anger? How often have you discussed your pay with your boss or a loan with your bank manager without being aware of your anxiety and the fact that you were breaking out in a sweat?

Whatever form your anxiety disorder takes, a specific fear, general anxiety, panic, phobia or a compulsion, you should ask yourself, "*Am I a total prisoner of my anxieties and fears?*" Being mindful is the way out of the prison, though mindfulness is not a forceful way to break out nor is it an effort of will (though you might need some will-power to do the exercises regularly!) Rather than a break-*out* it is a way of getting *inside* your mind and seeing what is happening there, noting your thoughts and feelings moment by moment, without negative reactions to your fears and anxieties. As you do this you come to realize that they are just thoughts which are coming and going all the time, but they *are not you.*

What happens when you practice mindfulness?

When you are doing either of the two mindfulness exercises in this chapter (there are many more but they don't concern us at the moment) your body is doing nothing or very little except the natural functions such as heartbeat and breathing. But a great deal is going on in your mind. Thoughts, feelings, emotions and anxieties and fears pass through it like a shoal of fish. Sometimes a particular "fish" will keep returning (remember the repetitive anxieties in Chapter 3?) but there is always movement and the scene is constantly changing.

You would certainly rather have peace in your mind than constant uproar and confusion (nothing unusual!) But the fishes keep coming and going...

When thoughts or feelings come up in your mind during the exercises, don't ignore them or suppress them, nor analyze or judge their content. Rather, you simply note any thoughts as they occur as best you can and observe them intentionally but non-judgmentally, moment by moment, simply as events in the field of your awareness. Paradoxically, this noting of thoughts and feelings that come and go in your mind and body can lead you to no longer getting caught up in them. You "ride" on them like a surfer on the waves rather than be tossed around by them. And that's the key that lets anxiety out of your life.

What does "non-judgmentally" mean here? It means not labeling the fish as "good", "bad" or not even "neutral". This allows you to simply let them swim by, and because they are not labeled, they become less powerful and threatening, even though some, such as the fears and anxieties, are highly emotionally charged. They will have less hold of your attention. If one should get "hooked" just remember it's only a thought, not the real thing. Are you, after all, frightened and anxious about your thoughts?

During the exercises you will get moments of comfort and relaxation, even though these may be brief to begin with, and you may notice that you are not *always* feeling anxious. You will realize that anxiety varies in intensity and comes and goes just like anything else in life and that it is only a temporary mental state.

But this is enough explanation. The only way really to understand and especially to *experience* mindfulness is to practice it. From being the result of an exercise it will become your "ordinary everyday mind".

Exercise 10. Body Scan

Do not do this exercise when you first of all start with your program, but only when you have made some progress with the others you have selected, as the anxieties might become too vivid. If they do, stop.

This exercise is best done lying on the floor (on a blanket). When you have done one scan take a short pause still lying down, then do another, as many times as you like.

During this exercise you will often be distracted by different thoughts, your anxieties or fears (the "fish") and for a moment you might forget all about the scan. All you need to do is to note what happened and return to the work in hand as often as you need – it will be quite often when you begin to do the exercise.

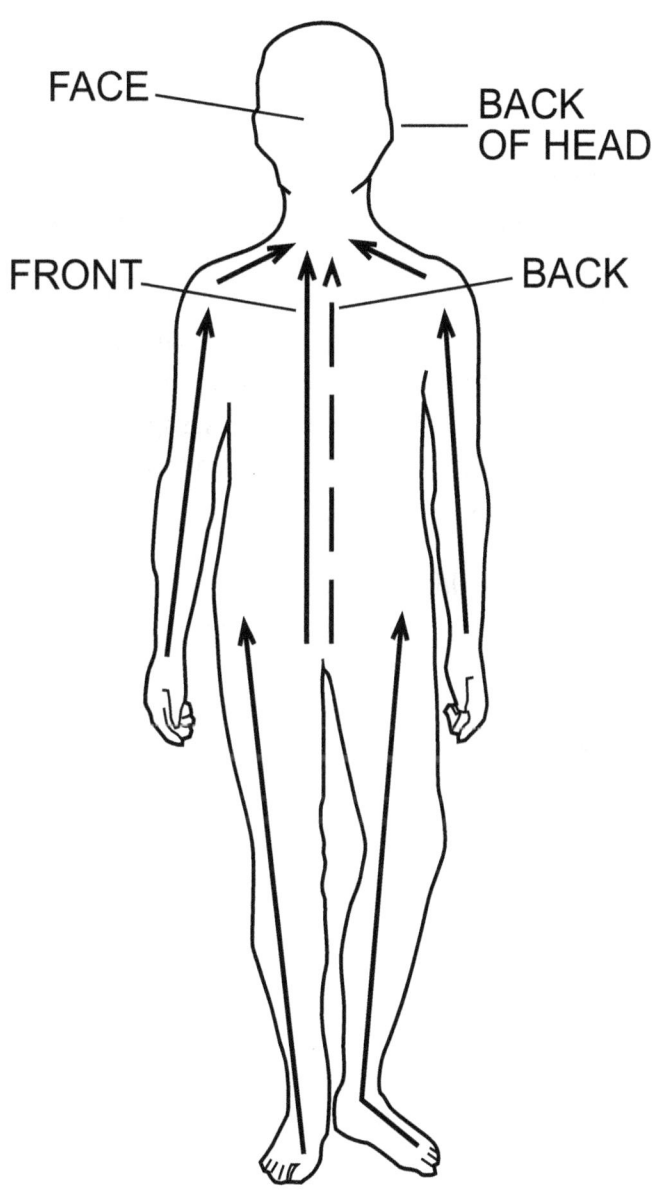

Scanning your body makes you aware of yourself in a way you may not have experienced before. It makes you very relaxed and reduces or even eliminates automatic reactions to your thoughts. Naturally it needs to be done regularly to bring the most benefit.

The scan is a gradual sweep of your attention from the toes to the top of your head, during which you will become aware of feelings and sensations in each part of your body you come to. Just note that the feelings are there. If you find a tension somewhere you can release it by making a slight movement, or if it is strong (as it might be in the shoulders, for example) tense the part as hard as you can for a second or so, then let go and feel how it relaxes.

Each sweep should take at least ten minutes. Instead of lying on the floor you can sit comfortably back on the couch. Close your eyes. Let your breathing be quite natural. If you don't think about your breathing it will flow gently and slow down.

- Begin by focusing your attention on the toes of your left foot, feel for any tensions there and release them. There are many other things you can feel down there – the pressure of your heels on the mattress, a cover or sheet over your toes, even the pain of a corn. Whatever you find, just be aware of it.

- Now bring your attention slowly up your left leg as far as your hip, still seeking out all the sensations you can find, such as the feel of your trousers or skirt on your skin.

- When you have finished with your left leg and are at the hip take a short pause, noting that you breathing is now smooth and regular, and then do a sweep from your right foot to the right hip. Pause there and then go to your left hand and up your arm to your shoulders. The hand needs particular attention, as it may be a little tense, specially the fingers. Pause and then scan along your right hand and up your arm.

- There are bound to be many sensations in your back, so now sweep slowly up from your buttocks (are they tense?) up to the shoulders. And do the same with the front of the body from the genital area to the neck.

- What can you feel in your shoulders and neck? Almost certainly tensions (let them go) but as well there will be the feel of clothes and the weight of your body against the mattress.

- Let's move to the face. The best method here is to wrinkle it up quite hard for a few seconds, then allow it to relax. You will get quite different feelings in it, which you can enjoy for a short while. The back of the head can also have tensions and certainly there will be feelings as it rests on the pillow. Explore these, just as you have been doing.

- Finish the exercise by imagining there is a hole at the top of your head. Breathe in quite deeply and visualize the air going right down to your feet. Pause, breathe slowly out right up your body, and then out through the hole.

Exercise 11. Slow walking

Do you think I'm going to teach you how to walk? After all, you learned that when you were a baby. But babies walk *mindfully,* giving their full attention to what they are doing, whereas we grown-ups do it automatically. Slow walking is a simple way of bringing mindfulness back into our lives. It is an exercise found in many cultures such as the Japanese Zen and the Chinese Chi Qong, and it is practiced by Buddhist monks, just as Buddha himself did.

Slow walking involves intentionally attending to all the sensations in your feet and legs and indeed your whole body, including your breathing, which should be natural. As in the case of Body Scan your attention is bound to be interrupted by many thoughts and these you can deal with in the same way, noting them and then returning to the walking. It's not a bad idea to stop walking when you have a distracting thought and start again when you have let it go.

The best place to do this exercise is in the open, where you have plenty of space and will be undisturbed. If this is not possible and you have to do it in a small room, do not walk in a circle, but clear a space to walk to and fro, turning slowly round when you need to.

- Stand with your feet shoulder breadth apart and parallel, the knees very slightly flexed. Place your hands on the belly, one over the other, and let them rest there being sure that you don't hunch your shoulders. Stay in this position for a few minutes, breathing naturally. Let your breathing come and go in this way throughout the exercise.

- Keep your eyes open or half closed, but do not close them completely, as you might lose your balance.

- Now you can begin to walk, but as slowly as possible. If you are in the garden the snails will rush past you! That's how slow.

- Keep the feet at the same distance apart, so that you sway very slightly with each step, and keep your hands on the belly. Move your right foot slowly forward in a short step and place the heel gently on the ground. Now roll the foot forwards until only the toes touch the ground and slowly let the heel down.

- Now move the left foot forward a short step, rest the heel on the ground, roll it until the toes are on the ground, and so on.

- You can do this exercise as long as you like, though 10 minutes may be enough to begin with. It is more strenuous than you might think, but mindfulness is not achieved without some effort.

Chapter 7

THE BREATHING MIND

The physical exercises in this chapter are not mere gymnastics or for body building. They are for "mind building", so should be done very slowly to give time to be aware of all the sensations such as muscles tensing and relaxing, the feeling of clothes on the skin and of course breathing.

Breathing is the link between our minds and our bodies, its rhythm and depth changing with our activities, thoughts and feelings. Our ability to concentrate, remain wakeful and ultimately be mindful depends on how we breathe. Breathing and anxiety affect each other greatly and so exercises which ensure correct breathing are an essential part of the Anxiety Relief Program. Breathing techniques will not cure anxiety, but they can help you to both reduce and avoid anxiety, phobia and panic. On the other hand, incorrect breathing can actually increase the tendency to anxiety and panic.

Even if you have never practiced mindfulness exercises before, you will know that the mind can be controlled by manipulating the breathing: Quiet breathing brings a quiet state of mind or if, when you feel like shouting with rage, you bate your breath, it will quieten you down and you will find your anger comes under control. In the other direction, anxiety and panic make many people have trouble breathing. They start to breathe faster and more shallowly, and in the extreme case they *hyperventilate*, i.e. overbreathe, and they may think they are having a heart attack. Actually, the worst that can happen is that they pass out, which is dangerous enough. A vicious circle begins when you feel unable to breathe (one of the symptoms of anxiety). You feel you are not getting enough air and an overwhelming wave of fear or panic can arise. But when you panic it just makes it harder to bring you breathing under control. A vicious circle indeed!

Let's do two experiments to see how state of mind and breathing influence each other (actually through the vegetative nervous system, but we won't go into the physiology).

NOTE: these experiments are simply to show the influence of mind over breathing and vice versa. You should not do them as exercises But if you do them occasionally you will gradually develop a persisting sense of whether you are breathing correctly or not.

- Imagine a stressful event (*not* your main anxiety). After even a short time you will find you are breathing faster and retain more air in the lungs than when relaxed and unstressed. If you've already had panic attacks, just the thought of another can be enough to change your breathing and quite probably start you on the way to another attack, even though you may not be aware of it. If you do feel you are getting one, stop and do Tanden-Do (Exercise 6, Chapter 4).

- With your eyes wide open, stare at, say, the corner of a building outside the window, a tree or even a picture on the wall. Stare at a fixed part of the object and don't allow you eyes to move. At the same time stop, or nearly stop, breathing and with your attention concentrated on that one point try to prevent ideas coming into your mind. You will find that this is really possible, especially if you practice it.

- Now breathe normally and try again to keep thoughts from your mind. It is as good as impossible!

Check your breathing

You can easily check whether you are breathing correctly:

Rest one hand on your upper chest and the other just below your navel. Inhale slowly and deeply through your nose, counting slowly to three. Notice which hand rises first when you inhale. If the upper hand rises first you are using upper chest breathing. If the lower hand rises first you are breathing with your belly. If both move at the same time you are using a mix of both.

Because we can control our breathing consciously to a degree, we can easily learn to adjust or modify it, as do singers, actors and instrument players.

Upper chest breathing is usually quick and shallow and results from anxiety; it does not allow enough oxygen to reach the organs, and so is distinctly unhealthy. Most of the time, though, our breathing is on "automatic pilot" and we don't think about it. Babies breathe with their tummies but the problems come when we learn chest breathing, often as children. This doesn't have bad effects immediately but eventually becomes a bad habit that can not only create the symptoms of anxiety but increases the likelihood of anxiety disorder. Therefore, if you are a confirmed chest breather, you should learn to become a belly breather, practicing until it is the normal thing for you. The exercises for this consist of mindful breathing, as opposed to automatic breathing.

Training yourself in mindful breathing

The Japanese Zen Masters have for many hundreds of years developed refined methods of training in belly breathing – "tanden" breathing as they call it. We have already met one method, Tanden-do (Exercise 6, Chapter 4), but we don't need to go as far as the Zen Masters, who have no anxiety problems but use tanden breathing to enter the state of "total stillness".

Exercise 12. Tanden breathing

This is one of the most important exercises in the Anxiety Relief Program. By practicing regularly (see Chapter 8, Putting your program together) you will greatly reduce your liability to any kind of anxiety disorder and even when you are quite justifiably anxious you will get fewer and milder symptoms of anxiety. Even if you are already a "tanden breather" the exercise will be of benefit.

The position shown here is used traditionally by Japanese women, though men also use it sometimes. In case you can't sit on your heels like the model, you could put a cushion between your buttocks and heels. Or you can sit on a stool or in one of the well-known meditation positions, making sure your back is straight.

Breathe in deeply through the nose, and deep down into the tanden. Imagine that the air circles round in your belly two or three times. The head remains upright. *Breathe slowly out* through the mouth but only when the breath "wants" to come.

The body automatically bends forwards when all the air has been breathed out. Wait for the next in-breath to come by itself. The head moves up again. Do this exercise 10 times. Do not rush it but allow the breath to take its own time.

Exercise 13. Breathing and movement

Start with the palms of your hands together, as in praying. Feel that you are balanced round the tanden.

Breathe in as you raise your hands above your head, keeping them together. Draw the breath deep into your belly.

Hold your breath and move the hands a little apart.

Breathe slowly out when you feel like it, at the same time lowering your hands.

Pause for a while, then raise your arms to the first position and repeat the breathing and movements.

Stand still and balance round the tanden for a minute or so.

Repeat the exercise 5 times.

Exercise 14. Breathing and movement

Breathe in down to the tanden, palms of the hands facing up. Pause, face your palms down, slowly breathe out slowly, as you lower your arms Repeat 5 times.

Exercise 15. Breathing and movement

Start with your arms out, palms facing upwards. *Breathe slowly and fully out* as you lower your arms, palms facing down. Stand still for a while, centered on the tanden, then raise your arms again, breathing in down to the tanden. Repeat 5 times.

Exercise 16. Breathing and stretching (1)

This and the next two exercises are particularly valuable after a session which includes the "TV" exercises 1, 2, 3, 4, 5, 8, 9, 10 or 11(Body Scan). Do one of them slowly, allowing ten minutes or so for it.

Stand straight with your arms by your sides.

Breathe deeply in as you raise your arms until your fingertips touch.

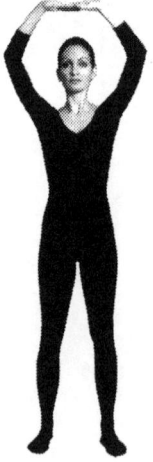

Hold your breath, then turn slowly to your left...

then to the right...

and finally face forwards. As you lower your arms breathe out from the tanden. Repeat 5 times.

Exercise 17. Breathing and stretching (2)

Slowly raise your arms above your head, *breathing in deeply*. Holding your breath, swing your body round, down and up in a circular movement and return to the first position. Breathe out, pause, breathe in, Repeat five times altogether.

Chapter 8

YOUR PROGRAM

The Way lies in the practice.

> Miamoto Musashi, greatest of all Japanese swordfighters, never beaten. (18th cent.)

You should first of all recognize that you are in charge and it is only by trying exercises out that you can find what is most suitable. Don't make the mistake of being too hasty about this, because to really feel the effect of an exercise you need to practice it quite a few times, particularly the ones with the TV and Body Scan.

There are altogether 18 different exercises in this book, and with their help you will be able to overcome your anxiety problem. They are described in the various chapters, so you will know which to do. The essential point is to try the ones relevant to the type of anxiety disorder you have and then do those that you feel comfortable with and which benefit you. Naturally you will not be able to decide for or against a particular exercise the first time you try it, so try several times.

When to do ARP sessions

It is absolutely necessary that you have some breathing and mindfulness practice every day. This need only be for ten minutes or so if that's all you've got time for The time and place for daily practice is naturally up to you. Make it a fixed point in your daily routine, not leaving it to "when I have time to spare".

The longer sessions are best left to weekends, when (presumably) you have more time and can find a quiet place for your practice. Again, do this routinely and make every effort not to miss a session out.

The object of making the practice sessions into a routine is that it integrates both mindfulness and the insights you get into your daily life and ensures continued progress.

What type of anxiety problem do you have?

Here is the first decision you need to make, because it affects which exercises you should do. To make sure, read the relevant chapters through again. It should not be hard to decide.

These are the possibilities:

Specific anxieties. These, as described in Chapter 2, "Facing up to anxiety", relate to only one (or possibly two) objects of anxiety. If not coped with this can, so to speak, "widen out" and affect your life as a whole, leading to the next type, which is

General anxiety. As explained in Chapter 3, "Don't worry – be happy", daily life becomes a state of worry, anxiety about almost anything, and fear, and is characterized by excessive thinking and dwelling on the "what ifs". Refer to your score in the questionnaire in chapter 3.

Panic attacks. There is also a questionnaire in Chapter 4, "Coping with panic" which you should look at again.

Phobias and compulsions. Chapter 5 deals with these extensively. You will certainly have no difficulty in recognizing a phobia or compulsion, but try not to hide them from yourself.

Daily practice and longer sessions

Daily practice, if it is only for ten minutes, can consist only of a breathing exercise. Try them out and choose the one you feel best with.

Longer sessions (week ends) should be in three stages, breathing 10-15 minutes, the main exercise (see below) for up to an hour and finally breathing and movement and stretching for ten minutes. This last stage brings you back to normal physical and mental activity.

1. Breathing exercises

Choose one from the following and practice it daily for a least a week. If at the end of this time you feel it does not suit you, try another.

(See the list of exercises in Chapter 9.)

Exercise 6. Tanden-Do, the way of the belly

Exercise 7. Slow breathing in six-second rhythm.

Exercise 12. Tanden breathing.

2. Main exercise for the session

Follow breathing exercise with a main exercise chosen from Chapters 2 or 3

Exercise 1. The "What would happen if...?" game.

Exercise 2. Putting the anxiety on tape.

Exercise 3. Viewing your anxieties.

Exercise 4. "Stopping the film" – first session.

Exercise 5. "Stopping the film" – second and further sessions.

Exercise 8. Putting your panic on tape.

3. Concluding exercises for the session

Exercises 13-15. Breathing and movement.

Exercises 16-17. Breathing and stretching.

Weekend practice sessions

Take advantage of weekends to do longer sessions. You will find them very beneficial. As a variation you could play some soft music. Take your time, taking pauses, maybe for a cup of coffee or a coke or a short stroll in the garden. If you are interrupted, just start again where you left off.

To begin, do the breathing exercise which you have found best in your daily practice for 10 minutes.

Now you have a choice. The main part of the session, which should last up to an hour, can be devoted either to Exercise 10, Body Scan (Chapter 6) OR the exercises in the chapter describing your particular form of anxiety problem. The recommendation is to do Body

Scan for at least four weeks, but only when you feel comfortable with the others. In this way you will have some experience of mindfulness before you start to work with your particular problem. Be sure you do some Breathing and Movement exercises at the end of your session to loosen you up.

Body Scan and Tanden-Do

Although Body Scan has been mentioned as a preliminary exercise it is in fact the final step in the ARP. Once you feel you have made good progress with the other exercises such as the films, treat yourself to a daily morning session of Body Scan, even if only for ten minutes or so. Follow this with some Breathing and Movement exercises to loosen up and your days will be free of the consequences of anxiety and you will be able to cope more successfully with life during the week.

It is also a very good idea to continue doing Tanden-Do daily even after your anxieties have been relieved. This will make sure that you keep up the good work.

Chapter 9

LIST OF EXERCISES

Chapter 2

Exercise 1. The "What would happen if...?" game.

Exercise 2. Putting the anxiety on tape.

Exercise 3. Viewing your anxieties.

Chapter 3

Exercise 4. "Stopping the film" – first session.

Exercise 5. "Stopping the film" – second and further sessions.

Chapter 4

Exercise 6. Tanden-Do, the way of the belly.

Exercise 7. Slow breathing in six-second rhythm.

Exercise 8. Putting your panic on tape.

Chapter 5

Exercise 9. Putting your phobia on tape.

Chapter 6

Exercise 10. Body Scan.

Exercise 11. Slow walking.

Chapter 7

Exercise 12. Tanden breathing.

Exercises 13-15. Breathing and movement.

Exercises 16-17. Breathing and stretching.

www.ingramcontent.com/pod-product-compliance
Lightning Source LLC
LaVergne TN
LVHW041630070426
835507LV00008B/549